CU00758444

by Iain Gray

Lang Syne

PUBLISHING

WRITING *to* REMEMBER

Lang Syne

PUBLISHING

WRITING *to* REMEMBER

79 Main Street, Newtongrange,
Midlothian EH22 4NA
Tel: 0131 344 0414   Fax: 0845 075 6085
E-mail: info@lang-syne.co.uk
www.langsyneshop.co.uk

Design by Dorothy Meikle
Printed by Printwell Ltd
© Lang Syne Publishers Ltd 2019

ISBN 978-1-85217-513-9

Ellis

MOTTO:
These things are not possible
without the deity.

CREST:
A naked female figure with her hair
flowing down to her waist.

NAME variations include:
Elis
Ellianson
Eliss
Elliss
Ellys

Chapter one:

The origins of popular surnames

by George Forbes and Iain Gray

***If you don't know where you came from, you won't know where you're going* is a frequently quoted observation and one that has a particular resonance today when there has been a marked upsurge in interest in genealogy, with increasing numbers of people curious to trace their family roots.**

Main sources for genealogical research include census returns and official records of births, marriages and deaths – and the key to unlocking the detail they contain is obviously a family surname, one that has been 'inherited' and passed from generation to generation.

No matter our station in life, we all have a surname – but it was not until about the middle of the fourteenth century that the practice of being identified by a particular surname became commonly established throughout the British Isles.

Previous to this, it was normal for a person to be identified through the use of only a forename.

But as population gradually increased and there were many more people with the same forename, surnames were adopted to distinguish one person, or community, from another.

Many common English surnames are patronymic in origin, meaning they stem from the forename of one's father – with 'Johnson,' for example, indicating 'son of John.'

It was the Normans, in the wake of their eleventh century conquest of Anglo-Saxon England, a pivotal moment in the nation's history, who first brought surnames into usage – although it was a gradual process.

For the Normans, these were names initially based on the title of their estates, local villages and chateaux in France to distinguish and identify these landholdings.

Such grand descriptions also helped enhance the prestige of these warlords and generally glorify their lofty positions high above the humble serfs slaving away below in the pecking order who had only single names, often with Biblical connotations as in Pierre and Jacques.

The only descriptive distinctions among the peasantry concerned their occupations, like 'Pierre the swineherd' or 'Jacques the ferryman.'

Roots of surnames that came into usage in England not only included Norman-French, but also Old French, Old Norse, Old English, Middle English, German, Latin, Greek, Hebrew and the Gaelic languages of the Celts.

The Normans themselves were originally Vikings, or 'Northmen', who raided, colonised and eventually settled down around the French coastline.

The had sailed up the Seine in their longboats in 900AD under their ferocious leader Rollo and ruled the roost in north eastern France before sailing over to conquer England in 1066 under Duke William of Normandy – better known to posterity as William the Conqueror, or King William I of England.

Granted lands in the newly-conquered England, some of their descendants later acquired territories in Wales, Scotland and Ireland – taking not only their own surnames, but also the practice of adopting a surname, with them.

But it was in England where Norman rule and custom first impacted, particularly in relation to the adoption of surnames.

This is reflected in the famous *Domesday Book*, a massive survey of much of England and Wales, ordered by William I, to determine who owned what, what it was worth and therefore how much they were liable to pay in taxes to the voracious Royal Exchequer.

Completed in 1086 and now held in the National Archives in Kew, London, 'Domesday' was an Old English word meaning 'Day of Judgement.'

This was because, in the words of one contemporary chronicler, "its decisions, like those of the Last Judgement, are unalterable."

It had been a requirement of all those English landholders – from the richest to the poorest – that they identify themselves for the purposes of the survey and for future reference by means of a surname.

This is why the *Domesday Book*, although written in Latin as was the practice for several centuries with both civic and ecclesiastical records, is an invaluable source for the early appearance of a wide range of English surnames.

Several of these names were coined in connection with occupations.

These include Baker and Smith, while Cooks, Chamberlains, Constables and Porters were to be found carrying out duties in large medieval households.

The church's influence can be found in names such as Bishop, Friar and Monk while the popular name of Bennett derives from the late fifth to mid-sixth century Saint Benedict, founder of the Benedictine order of monks.

The early medical profession is represented by Barber, while businessmen produced names that include Merchant and Sellers.

Down at the village watermill, the names that cropped up included Millar/Miller, Walker and Fuller, while other self-explanatory trades included Cooper, Tailor, Mason and Wright.

Even the scenery was utilised as in Moor, Hill, Wood and Forrest – while the hunt and the chase supplied names that include Hunter, Falconer, Fowler and Fox.

Colours are also a source of popular surnames, as in Black, Brown, Gray/Grey, Green and White, and would have denoted the colour of the clothing the person habitually wore or, apart from the obvious exception of 'Green', one's hair colouring or even complexion.

The surname Red developed into Reid, while

Blue was rare and no-one wanted to be associated with yellow.

Rather self-important individuals took surnames that include Goodman and Wiseman, while physical attributes crept into surnames such as Small and Little.

Many families proudly boast the heraldic device known as a Coat of Arms, as featured on our front cover.

The central motif of the Coat of Arms would originally have been what was borne on the shield of a warrior to distinguish himself from others on the battlefield.

Not featured on the Coat of Arms, but highlighted on page three, is the family motto and related crest – with the latter frequently different from the central motif.

Adding further variety to the rich cultural heritage that is represented by surnames is the appearance in recent times in lists of the 100 most common names found in England of ones that include Khan, Patel and Singh – names that have proud roots in the vast sub-continent of India.

Echoes of a far distant past can still be found in our surnames and they can be borne with pride in commemoration of our forebears.

Chapter two:

Ancient roots

A name that has been present in the British Isles from the earliest times, 'Ellis' has truly Biblical roots, deriving as it does from the Hebrew personal name 'Elijah', or the Greek 'Elias' – denoting 'Jehovah is God' and referring to the prophet Elijah.

This was the great figure of the Old Testament who championed the God of Israel against other gods.

Also a popular forename, as a surname it first came into vogue in the wake of the Norman Conquest of 1066 – but, in common with many other surnames found in England today, those who would come to bear it were of ancient Anglo-Saxon roots.

This means that flowing through the veins of many bearers of the name today may well be the blood of those Germanic tribes who invaded and settled in the south and east of the island of Britain from about the early fifth century.

Known as the Anglo-Saxons, they were composed of the Jutes, from the area of the Jutland

Peninsula in modern Denmark, the Saxons from Lower Saxony, in modern Germany and the Angles from the Angeln area of Germany.

It was the Angles who gave the name 'Engla land', or 'Aengla land' – better known as 'England.'

They held sway in what became England from approximately 550 to 1066, with the main kingdoms those of Sussex, Wessex, Northumbria, Mercia, Kent, East Anglia and Essex.

Whoever controlled the most powerful of these kingdoms was tacitly recognised as overall 'king' – one of the most noted being Alfred the Great, King of Wessex from 871 to 899.

It was during his reign that the famous *Anglo-Saxon Chronicle* was compiled – an invaluable source of Anglo-Saxon history – while Alfred was designated in early documents as *Rex Anglorum Saxonum*, King of the English Saxons.

Other important Anglo-Saxon works include the epic *Beowulf* and the seventh century *Caedmon's Hymn*.

The Anglo-Saxons, meanwhile, had usurped the power of the indigenous Britons – who referred to them as 'Saeson' or 'Saxones.'

It is from this that the Scottish Gaelic term

for 'English people' of 'Sasannach' derives, the Irish Gaelic 'Sasanach' and the Welsh 'Saeson.'

But the death knell of Anglo-Saxon supremacy was sounded with the Conquest, led by Duke William of Normandy, and the death at the battle of Hastings of Harold II, last of the Anglo-Saxon kings.

William was declared king, and the complete subjugation of his Anglo-Saxon subjects followed.

Within an astonishingly short space of time, Norman manners, customs and law were imposed on England – laying the basis for what subsequently became established 'English' custom and practice.

But beneath the surface, old Anglo-Saxon culture was not totally eradicated.

Some aspects were absorbed into those of the Normans, while faint echoes of the Anglo-Saxon past is still seen today in the form of popular surnames such as Ellis.

Earliest records of the name, in what are now some redundant forms, are first found in Yorkshire, with a William Elyas recorded there in 1200 – while much further south, a William Elis is recorded in Lincolnshire in 1202 and a Robert Elys in Sussex in 1250.

Bearers of the name figure prominently in what is the frequently turbulent history of England.

During the bitter seventeenth century English Civil War, Clement Ellis was from a prominent Royalist family.

The Catholic monarch Charles I had incurred the wrath of Parliament by his insistence on the 'divine right' of kings, and added to this was Parliament's fear of Catholic 'subversion' against the state and the king's stubborn refusal to grant demands for religious and constitutional concessions.

Matters came to a head with the outbreak of the Civil War in 1642, with Parliamentary forces, known as the New Model Army and commanded by Oliver Cromwell and Sir Thomas Fairfax, arrayed against the Royalist army of the king.

In what became an increasingly bloody and complex conflict, spreading to Scotland and Ireland and with rapidly shifting loyalties on both sides, the king was eventually captured and executed in January of 1649 on the orders of Parliament.

Born in 1633 in Rose Castle, Cumberland, Clement Ellis's father was the Royalist Captain Philip Ellis who, as steward of the castle on behalf of the Bishop of Carlisle, successfully defended it for four years against the Parliamentary forces.

It was as thanks for his loyalty that Royalist

sources provided money for his son to be educated at Queen's College, Oxford.

Ordained as a clergyman four years before the Restoration of Charles II in 1660, Clement Ellis later became private chaplain to the Duke of Newcastle. Also a noted poet and author of works that include *England's Brave Gentlemen*, he died in 1700.

By the very nature of Civil War, family loyalties and allegiances were ripped apart as Parliamentarians and Royalists arrayed themselves against one another on the battlefield.

Although not related to Clement Ellis, but sharing the same proud surname, Sir William Ellis was the prominent Parliamentarian, lawyer and judge born in 1609 in Grantham, Lincolnshire.

Educated at Christ's College, Cambridge and qualifying as a lawyer in 1634, he was later elected to the House of Commons as Member of Parliament (MP) for Boston, Lincolnshire, while in 1654 he was appointed Solicitor-General under Oliver Cromwell.

It was in this role that he was instrumental in the prosecution and subsequent beheading of two Royalists found guilty of attempting to assassinate Cromwell; he died in 1680.

Towards the end of the tumultuous seventeenth

century, another Sir William Ellis's support for the Royal House of Stuart led to his downfall in the wake of what is known as the Glorious Revolution of 1688.

This was when the Catholic James II (James VII of Scotland) was forced to flee into exile and was replaced on the throne by the Protestant William of Orange and his wife Mary.

Ellis, who had been a member of the ill-fated James's Privy Council, later joined the monarch in his exile in France, serving as his secretary.

Following the death of James in 1701, he acted as treasurer to his son, James III, known as the Old Pretender, at his court-in-exile in Rome; it was here that he died in 1732.

Continuing the tradition of bearers of the Ellis name holding high office, Welbore Ellis was the British statesman born in 1713.

The son of the Rev. Welbore Ellis, Bishop of Kildare and Bishop of Meath, he was raised to the Peerage of the United Kingdom eight years before his death in 1802 as 1st Baron Mendip, of Mendip in the County of Somerset.

This was after having served in a number of posts that included Secretary of the Colonies during the American War of Independence of 1775 to 1783.

Born in 1799, Charles Augustus Ellis, 6th Baron Howard de Walden and 2nd Baron Seaford, was the British politician and diplomat who held a number of prominent posts that included Joint Under-Secretary of State for Foreign Affairs and the grandly titled Envoy Extraordinary and Minister Plenipotentiary to the Court of Stockholm.

He died in 1868, while one of his descendants was the colourful John Osmael Scott-Ellis, 9th Baron de Walden and 5th Baron Seaford.

Born in 1912, he later inherited Dean Castle, in Kilmarnock, East Ayrshire – donating it along with its impressive collection of arms and armour to the people of the town in 1975.

A Thoroughbred racehorse owner and trainer and a steward of the Jockey Club, one of his many racing successes was winning the 1985 Epsom Derby with Slip Anchor.

He died in 1999, while one of his decidedly odd claims to fame goes back to 1931 when he was living for a time in Munich.

Buying a car shortly after arriving in the German city, he accidently knocked down a pedestrian – none other than Adolf Hitler, future leader of the Third Reich.

Chapter three:

Honours and distinction

Bearers of the Ellis name have gained particular distinction in fields ranging from engineering and architecture to the sciences and medicine.

Born in Parkman, Maine, in 1876, Charles Alton Ellis was the American mathematician and structural engineer who played a key role in the design of San Francisco's magnificent Golden Gate Bridge, named by the American Society of Civil Engineers as one of the Wonders of the Modern World.

He died in 1949, twelve years after the bridge was opened.

On British shores, Peter Ellis, born in 1808 and who died in 1888, was the English architect famed for landmark works in Liverpool that include the Oriel Chambers.

Also in the creative world of architecture, Sir Bertram Clough Williams-Ellis was the English-born Welsh architect best known as the creator of the Italianate village of Portmeirion, in North Wales.

Awarded the Military Cross following service

with the Welsh Guards during the First World War, it was in the 1920s that he began work on Portmeirion – famously used as the location in the mid-1960s for the cult British television series *The Prisoner*.

Born in 1883 in Gayton, Northamptonshire but moving to Wales with his family when aged four, he died in 1978 – six years after receiving a knight-hood for his services to architecture.

Responsible for pioneering work on the magnetic spectrum of beta-rays that greatly enhanced the understanding of nuclear structure, Sir Charles Ellis was the British physicist born in 1895 in Hampstead, London.

He had been aged 19 and on holiday in Germany when the First World War broke out in 1914.

Interred in a POW camp along with other British nationals who had been caught up in Germany, he struck up a friendship with fellow internee James Chadwick – later the recipient of a Nobel Prize for his work on the discovery of the neutron.

It was Chadwick who inspired Ellis to pursue a scientific career. Studying natural sciences at Trinity College, Cambridge and graduating in the early 1920s, he became engaged in research work at the Cavendish Laboratory, in Cambridge.

This was where Chadwick and fellow physicist Sir Eric Rutherford were also engaged in research. While they carried out ground-breaking research into alpha radioactivity and alpha particles, Ellis conducted research into both beta and gamma radiation – ultimately leading to the discovery of the neutrino.

Scientific adviser from 1943 to 1946 to the British Army Council, he died in 1980.

Reaching for the heavens, George Ellis, born in 1939 in Johannesburg, is the leading South African cosmologist who, along with British physicist Professor Stephen Hawking, co-authored the 1973 *The Large Scale Structure of Space-Time*.

A former president of the International Society for Science and Religion, he has also held the post of professor of complex systems in the department of mathematics and applied mathematics at the University of Cape Town.

In the equally complex world of secret codes and communications, James Henry Ellis was the British engineer and mathematician involved in the development of what is known as 'public-key cryptography.'

It was while working at the Government

Communications Headquarters (GCHQ) in Cheltenham that in 1970 he developed a technique for 'encrypting', or keeping secret from outsiders, certain telephone or computer communications.

His work was so secret that it was not until a month before his death in 1997, at the age of 73, that the Government publicly acknowledged his contribution.

Still in the world of electronic communications, James Ellis was the American computer scientist who, along with Tom Truscott, established the system known as 'Usenet'.

This was in 1980, enabling users to read and post messages – known as 'articles', or 'posts' – to one or more categories known as 'newsgroups.'

Born in 1956 in Nashville, Tennessee, he died in 2001.

In the world of medicine, Frank Ellis was a pioneer in the field of treatment of cancer by radiation therapy.

Appointed the first director of the radiotherapy department at the Royal London Hospital in 1943, he established the radiotherapy department at the Churchill Hospital, Oxford, seven years later.

A recipient of the Gold Medal of the Royal College of Radiologists and a past president of the

British Institute of Radiology, he died in 2006 at the age of 100.

One particularly tragic bearer of the Ellis name was Ruth Ellis, who holds the unenviable 'distinction' of having been the last woman to be hanged for murder in the United Kingdom after being convicted of murdering her abusive lover.

Born Ruth Neilson in 1926 in Rhyl, Wales, the third of six children, the family moved to Basingstoke when she was a young girl.

Working in a succession of lowly paid factory and clerical jobs after leaving school, she turned to nude modelling work, and later as a nightclub hostess and prostitute.

In 1950 she married a 41-year-old divorced dentist, George Ellis, but the marriage proved disastrous as Ellis frequently subjected her to violent abuse.

The couple soon separated, and in 1953 Ruth became hostess of a London nightclub, the Carroll Club, where she proved immensely popular among a clientele that included a number of celebrities.

Among them was the former public school boy David Blakely, three years her junior and an aspiring motor racing driver. He moved in with her to her flat above the club – she unaware at the time that he was already engaged to be married.

The relationship and Ruth's life in general soon spiralled out of control – with Blakely causing her to miscarry the child she was carrying when he punched her in the stomach during a drunken rage.

Matters went from bad to worse when she lost her nightclub job.

Moving in with Desmond Cussens, a former RAF pilot, who appears to have treated her with respect and kindness, she nevertheless was still besotted with Blakely.

On Easter Sunday of 1955 she tracked him down to a public house in the Hampstead area of London. As he exited the bar and approached his car, she gunned him down with a number of shots from a revolver – the exact reasons for the action never satisfactorily explained.

Convicted of his murder after a sensational trial at the Old Bailey in June of 1955, she was sentenced to hang.

This caused a public outcry, with the matter at one point being discussed in the Cabinet and a petition signed by 50,000 people asking for clemency delivered to the Home Office.

But it was all to no avail – she was hanged in Holloway Prison on July 12.

The last execution of a woman in the United Kingdom, the Ellis case is regarded as having strengthened public support for the abolition of the death penalty – and it was in 1964 that the last execution in the UK was carried out.

There have been a number of unsuccessful attempts over the years for Ruth Ellis to be granted a pardon in the light of new evidence that was not available to the Old Bailey jury in 1955, while she is portrayed by the actress Miranda Richardson in the 1985 film *Dance with a Stranger*.

Chapter four:

On the world stage

First taking professionally to the stage at the age of 21 with the Ulster Theatre Group after having trained at the Old Vic Theatre School, Bristol, James Ellis is the veteran British actor born in Belfast in 1931.

Although best known for his role from 1962 to 1968 in the television police series *Z-Cars*, he is also known for popular roles in other British television series that include *Ballykissangel*, *In Sickness and in Health* and *The Bill*.

A noted writer of both poetry and prose, he is also a translator – with a selection of his adaptations from French works broadcast on BBC Radio in 2007.

Born in London in 1955, **Jack Ellis** is the English actor best known for his roles in popular television series that include *Coronation Street*, *Heartbeat*, *Where the Heart Is*, *Inspector Morse* and *Lewis*.

Known for her role of Joy from 1970 to 1972 in the American children's television series *The Bugaloos*, **Caroline Ellis** is the English actress, born in London in 1950, whose British television credits include the comedy series *Only Fools and Horses*.

Also on the television screen, **Aunjanue Ellis**, born in 1969 in San Francisco, is the American actress whose many credits include *The Mentalist*, *True Blood* and *Missing*.

Back to British television screens, **Tom Ellis**, born in 1979 in Cardiff, is the Welsh actor, married since 2006 to the actress Tamzin Outhwaite, whose credits include *EastEnders*, *Pulling* and *Miranda*.

Best known as a presenter in the 1970s and 1980s of the British children's programmes *Blue Peter* and *Jigsaw*, **Janet Ellis** was born in 1955 in Chatham, Kent.

Married from 1977 to 1984 to the television director Robin Bextor, she is the mother of the singer, songwriter and model **Sophie Ellis-Bextor**.

Born in 1979 in Hounslow, London, she first came to prominence in the late 1990s as the lead singer of the band Theaudience. Now a successful solo artist, she has enjoyed hits with albums that include her 2001 *Read My Lips* and the 2011 *Make a Scene*.

Now resident in Britain, Alfred Ellis is the renowned American saxophonist, composer and arranger better known by his nickname of **Pee Wee Ellis**.

Born in 1941 in Bradenton, Florida, and having worked with a range of artistes who include George Benson, Esther Phillips and Van Morrison, he is best known for his work from 1965 to 1969 with soul artist James Brown in the James Brown Revue.

It was with Brown that he co-wrote hits that include *Cold Sweat* and *Say It Loud – I'm Black and I'm Proud*.

Born in Kingston in 1938, **Alton Ellis** was the Jamaican musician known as "The Godfather of Rocksteady."

Recognised as a prime innovator of the rocksteady genre of music, he enjoyed international hits with albums that include his 1967 *Mr Soul of Jamaica*, the 1970 *Second Coming* and, from 2000, *Change My Mind*.

An inductee of the International Reggae Hall of Music and a recipient of Jamaica's Order of Distinction for his services to music, he died in 2008, while he was the older brother of the reggae musician **Hortense Ellis**.

Born in 1941, she died in 2000, having

enjoyed hits throughout the 1970s that include *Unexpected Places* and *Down Town Ting*.

Back to British shores, **Kerry Ellis**, born in 1979 in Haughley, Suffolk, is the singer and actress with stage musical credits that include the 2001 revival of *My Fair Lady*, *We Will Rock You*, *Les Miserables*, *Miss Saigon* and *Chess*. Her solo album, *Anthems*, was released in 2010.

In a much different musical genre, **Osian Ellis** is the Welsh harpist and composer particularly known for his collaboration for a time with the composer Benjamin Britten.

Born in 1928 in Flintshire and a former principal harpist with the London Symphony Orchestra and a recipient of the CBE, he is also the author of a number of books that include his 1991 *The Story of the Harp in Wales*.

From the world of music to the equally creative world of the written word, **Bret Easton Ellis**, born in Los Angeles in 1964, is the best-selling American novelist and short story writer whose debut novel, *Less Than Zero*, was published when he was aged 21.

The novel was later adapted for a film of the same name, as was his 1991 *American Psycho*.

On Australian shores, **Bob Ellis** is the

journalist, writer, filmmaker and political commentator who's 1978 *Newsfront* won an Australian Film Institute Award for Best Screenplay; born in 1942 in Lismore, New South Wales, he has also written speeches for a number of the country's Labor Party leaders who have included Bob Carr and Paul Keating.

Not only a novelist but also a historian, **Peter Berresford Ellis** is the prolific British author born in 1943 in Coventry.

A leading authority on Celtic subjects and author of books that include the 1968 *Wales: a Nation Again* and the 1974 *The Cornish Language and its Literature*, he also writes the *Sister Fidelma* series of mystery novels under the pseudonym of Peter Tremayne.

A Fellow of the Royal Society of Antiquities of Ireland and the Royal Historical Society, he also writes under the pseudonym of Peter Macalan.

A mathematician and also a pioneer in the field of the study of languages known as philology, **Alexander Ellis** was born in 1814 in Hoxton, Middlesex.

His birth surname was 'Sharpe', but he adopted his mother's maiden name as a youth as a condition of receiving considerable financial support from one of his mother's wealthy Ellis relatives.

Educated at Trinity College, Cambridge, and obtaining degrees in mathematics and the classics, he went on to pursue his fascination with language and phonetics.

This resulted in applying what was known as the Dialect Test across Britain – through which he identified 42 different dialects in England and the Scottish Lowlands.

The inspiration for George Bernard Shaw's character of Professor Henry Higgins in his play *Pygmalion*, later adapted for both the stage musical and the film *My Fair Lady*, he died in 1890.

Combining literature with art, **Carson Ellis** is the award-winning American book illustrator born in 1975 in Portland, Oregon.

Her best known works, in the world of children's books, include the 2009 *The Composer is Dead*, written by Lemony Snicket, and the 2011 *Wildwood*, with Colin Meloy.

Bearers of the Ellis name have also excelled in the highly competitive world of sport.

In the swimming pool, Kathleen Ellis, better known as **Kathy Ellis**, born in 1946 in Trenton, New

Jersey, is the American swimmer who won two gold medals at the 1964 Olympics in Tokyo.

These were in the 4x100-metres freestyle relay and the 4x100-metres medley relay, while she also won bronze medals in the 100-metres freestyle and 100-metres butterfly events.

The recipient of an award from the International Swimming Hall of Fame, **Jim Ellis** is the American coach who in 1971 formed the first African-American swimming team.

Known as PDR (Pride, Determination, Resilience), it has gone on to produce top African-American swimmers who include Michael Normont, the first black swimmer on the U.S. national team; born in 1948, Ellis is the subject of the 2007 biopic *Pride*.

From the swimming pool to the boxing ring, **Jimmy Ellis** is the American retired boxer, born in 1940 in Louisville, Kentucky, who held the World Heavyweight Championship title from 1968 to 1970.

On the fields of European football, **Arthur Ellis** was the noted English referee who officiated at the 1950, 1954 and 1958 World Cups. Born in 1914 in Halifax, West Yorkshire, he died in 1999 – after having also become well known for his role of referee in the television game show *It's A Knockout*.

In the rough and tumble that is the game of rugby, **Andy Ellis**, born in 1984 in Christchurch, is the New Zealand scrum-half who, in addition to playing for clubs that include the Crusaders in the Super Rugby League, made his debut with the national team in 2006.

One of the most famous names in the history of rugby is that of **William Webb Ellis** – reputed to have 'invented' the game while a pupil at Rugby School, Warwickshire.

Born in 1806 in Salford, Lancashire and moving with his mother to Rugby following the death of his father, it is in 1823 that he is famed for having inadvertently laid the foundation for what would become the game of rugby.

This was during a school football match when, against the rules of the game, he caught the ball in his arms and ran with it.

A plaque erected at Rugby School in 1895 explains his role in the creation of rugby by stating: "This commemorates the exploits of William Webb Ellis who, with a fine disregard for the rules of football as played in his time, first took the ball in his hands and ran with it, thus originating the distinctive feature of the rugby game."

Later studying at Brasenose College, Oxford, and becoming an Anglican clergyman, he died in 1872 – while his role in the creation of the game is commemorated through the William Webb Ellis Cup, presented to winners of the Rugby World Cup.

One particularly daring bearer of the proud name of Ellis was the pioneering aviator **Frank H. Ellis**.

Born in Nottingham, he was aged 16 when he immigrated with his family to Canada in 1912.

Settling in Calgary, Alberta, he constructed and flew his own biplane only two years later – while in 1919 he became the first person to make a parachute jump over Canadian soil.

Author of a number of works on the history of aviation, including his *Canada's Flying Heritage*, he was awarded the Medal of Service of the Order of Canada seven years before his death in 1979.